WHEN I WAS YOUNG
EARLY 20TH CENTURY

RUTH THOMSON
MEETS
NANCY EMERY (NÉE GILLAH)

WATTS BOOKS
LONDON · SYDNEY

Nancy Emery was born in 1906 in the small village of Wilberfoss in Yorkshire. After a country childhood, she went to London to train as a teacher. She taught in the East End of London for two years. In 1931 she left teaching and travelled to India to marry an English engineer working for a British firm.

They lived in India for 18 years in Bombay and Calcutta. They had one son. The family moved back to Britain in 1949 and settled in Cheshire. When he retired they moved to St Albans.

Her son was killed in a tragic climbing accident in 1963. His daughter, Mary, works as a teacher in Putney.

Her husband died in 1983. Nancy continues to live in St Albans.

CONTENTS

Me and my family 8

Our house 10

Family life 12

Going to York 20

Sundays 22

Visitors 24

Around the village 26

School 28

High days and holidays 32

Growing up 36

In the news 38

Things to do 42

Glossary 44

Index 45

Me and my family

"The seventh child"

I was born in Wilberfoss, a little village a few miles east of York, in 1906 and christened Nancy Elizabeth Gillah. I was the seventh of nine children — all girls.

We were a happy family. We had plenty to eat and we enjoyed one another's company. Our life was our home and the village. We didn't think much about the outside world. In those days, there was no television, no radio, no telephone and no cars or buses.

Me aged four.

King Edward VII was on the throne when Nancy was born.

My family in 1916. I'm the one on the far right, sitting down.

My youngest sister, Mary, with a portrait of our grandmother, Ann Swann.

My family tree.

Henry Quarton Gillah
1833-1912

= Ann Swann
1827-1879

John Sherbourne

= Ann

John Henry
1869-1940

Frederick William
1873-1966

Arthur George
1872-1930

= Mary
1873-1922

May	Swannie	Marjorie	Kathleen	Lillie	Sylvia	Nancy	Joyce	Mary
1893—1984	1895-1973	1897-1985	1899-1975	1901—1925	1905—1987	b. 1906	b. 1907	b. 1911

Our house

"I shared a room"

We lived at Hope House, Middle Street. It was double-fronted, with an enormous garden at the back. The front room on the right was our playroom. The front room on the left was the living room. Down a passage was a big kitchen with a range, and two dairies. In one dairy, we kept the crockery and all the pies and puddings. In the other dairy, which was cooler, we kept big bowls of milk and eggs as well as a churn for making butter.

Upstairs were five bedrooms. My parents had the biggest one. I shared a room with my two younger sisters, Joyce and Mary. I had a single bed and they shared a double bed. My two elder sisters shared another bedroom and two live-in maids shared the bedroom next door. There was a spare bedroom for when one of us was ill.

Hope House as it was in my childhood.

Hope House today. Now it has electricity, running water and central heating. The wash-house is a workshop. The stables and cowsheds have been knocked down and eight new houses built on the site.

Oil lamps like this were used in homes before electric lights were introduced. In towns, many homes had gas lighting.

Each bedroom had a washstand and a chamber pot. We had no running water in the house and the lavatory was outside. There were oil lamps in the downstairs rooms, but we went to bed by candlelight.

There were several outbuildings next to the house. There was a stable for our horse, Mabel, and two coach-houses for the trap and the gig. There was a wash-house with a big copper, a coal store, a pigsty and some cowsheds.

There was a pump outside where we fetched water for drinking and cooking. In the winter, it was covered with sacking to stop the water from freezing. There were also three corrugated iron tanks at the corners of the house, to collect soft rainwater off the roof for washing. The water was heated in huge pans over a coal fire or in the wash-house copper.

Most people had washstands like this in their bedrooms. They brought hot water upstairs in the jug and poured it into the basin for washing themselves.

Our family in the garden. I'm sitting on the bench next to my father.

Family life

"A strict household routine"

I adored my mother. She was very tiny — her shoes were only size 2. She was always busy. I can't ever remember her sitting down, except to do the mending — and there was always a lot of that to do — and to play hymns on the piano on Sunday evenings.

Mother followed a strict household routine. On Mondays, it was always washday. Mrs Blackburn, a widow, used to come and help. The washing was done, all by hand, in the wash-house.

The water came from the pump. It was heated in the enormous copper and ladled into a big tub. Everything was mangled and hung out to dry on lines in the garden. If it was wet, the clothes were dried in front of the fire on a clothes-horse. We were such a big family, you can imagine what hard work washday was.

My mother with May, my eldest sister.

Washing equipment. The washing was put with hot soapy water in the poss-tub, and swished around with a posser to loosen the dirt. This photograph shows several sorts of possers.

The clean wet clothes were put through a mangle to squeeze out the water and smooth them.

Everyone had at least two flat irons, so one could be heated, while the other was being used.

Butter making. Once the cream had turned to butter in the churn, it was rolled in a butter worker, which squeezed out any moisture.

Tuesday was ironing day. Mrs Blackburn used those heavy flat irons that had to be heated on the kitchen range. It took her all day to starch and iron everything.

Wednesday and Thursday were baking days. Mother made fruit pies, cakes, jam tarts, all sorts of wonderful pastries and, of course, all our own bread. There was always a wonderful smell in the house on baking days.

We also made our own butter. Milk was brought from the farm in buckets and put in large flat bowls overnight. The cream was skimmed off the top of the milk and put into a churn. When the barrel was turned, the cream changed slowly into butter.

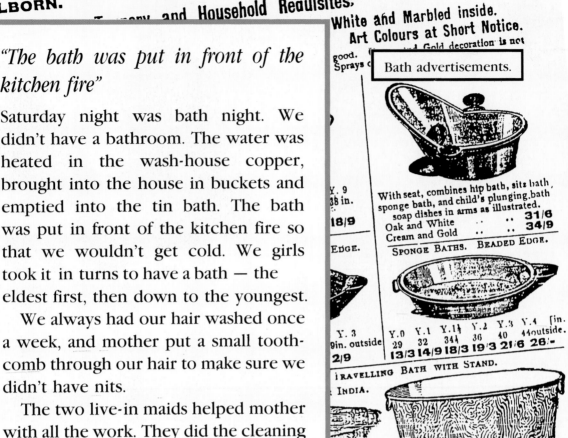

"The bath was put in front of the kitchen fire"

Saturday night was bath night. We didn't have a bathroom. The water was heated in the wash-house copper, brought into the house in buckets and emptied into the tin bath. The bath was put in front of the kitchen fire so that we wouldn't get cold. We girls took it in turns to have a bath — the eldest first, then down to the youngest.

We always had our hair washed once a week, and mother put a small tooth-comb through our hair to make sure we didn't have nits.

The two live-in maids helped mother with all the work. They did the cleaning and polishing, and helped with the cooking, baking and washing up.

They wore a uniform. In the mornings, when they were doing the dirty chores, they wore a cotton dress. In the afternoons, they wore a black dress with a starched white apron.

Bath advertisements.

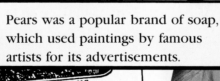

Pears was a popular brand of soap, which used paintings by famous artists for its advertisements.

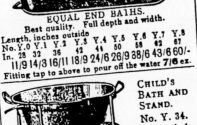

Chickens and geese were plucked by hand.

In 1911, over one million girls and women were employed as domestic servants.

On rainy days at school, when it was too wet to come home for lunch, one of the maids would bring us a basket laden with sandwiches, pies and fruits. We adored lunch at school; we couldn't wait for rainy days!

Other people worked for us as well. Miss Poole came to pluck the chickens in the wash-house. All the feathers were sorted and cleaned and kept in a bag to use for stuffing cushions, pillows and eiderdowns. If she was in the mood, Miss Poole would tell us our fortunes in tea leaves.

Wilkinson did the odd jobs. He looked after the horses, did the gardening and tended the fruit and vegetables. Every morning, he raked the gravel in the drive.

"Buying and selling cattle"

My father worked with his brothers and my grandfather. They were cattle dealers. Father spent most of his time buying and selling cattle at market fairs all around Yorkshire.

Once a week, he hired a drover to walk cattle (thirty or forty at a time) from Wilberfoss to York. The cattle would rest in a field just outside York for the day before the market. My father had special cutters for marking his cattle, so he knew which were his. Every dealer had a different mark.

The sales were all private. Once a buyer had fixed a price, he agreed the sale by shaking hands with the seller. The drovers would hang around waiting to be hired to drive the cattle back home again. Father knew which drovers were good. He never employed one who hit the cattle or drove them too fast.

The cattle were put in one of our fields ready for the next market in another nearby town, such as Malton or Driffield. Sometimes Father sold one or two to the butcher in the village.

My father dressed very smartly. I never saw him wear anything but a suit. He always wore a tie-pin and a watch-chain and a fresh flower in his buttonhole.

5

Each evening, when Father came home, he would call for his slippers and then settle down to read the Yorkshire Post.

Cattle being driven to York market.

The old livestock market. During the First World War, people had to give up many of their horses for the army to use. These horses are waiting to be transported by train.

The old market was demolished in 1971. A new, covered one was built on the outskirts of the city.

The farm

"A big supper of pigs' fry"

Our farm and garden provided us with a lot of our food. We grew apples and pears and all our vegetables in the back garden. We kept hens for eggs and chickens to eat.

We fattened up pigs for winter in the pigsty beside the house. I hated it when a pig was killed. I remember hiding in my bed with my head under the eiderdown, so that I couldn't hear the squealing so much. There was always a big supper of pigs' fry (the liver and offal) straight after the killing.

In the fields behind the house, we grew potatoes and corn. At potato-picking time, we little ones brought the pickers their bread, cheese and tea. We called it 'taking the drinkings'. All the potatoes were put in a great heap in the yard and covered with soil, to protect them from frost and snow in the winter.

Horses pulled the ploughs, which were guided by a ploughman. It was quite an art to plough in straight lines.

During the First World War, when many men went away to fight, women had to help with potato picking. My older sisters helped too. We smaller ones brought the drinkings — I'm the one in the middle.

A steam-powered threshing machine, which separated corn seed from straw.

Father hired men to do the ploughing, sowing and harvesting of the corn. After the harvest, we had great fun gleaning for the last ears of corn, which we threw to the chickens.

The great event in autumn was the day when the threshing machine came trundling through the white gate into the stackyard. It was a great monster of a machine. Every farmer hired it in turn. It must have been very hot work lifting the corn into the machine, so there was always a lot of tea drunk.

The corn seed was stored in sacks and was used for feeding our hens. The hay and straw were built into stacks. When the stacks got lower as the straw was used for bedding for our pigs and horses, we had great fun sliding down them.

Hay and straw stacks were built with thatched roofs to keep them dry.

Going to York

"My favourite shop was the Penny Bazaar"

On Saturdays, father and mother took the pony and trap and went to York. We children took it in turns to go with them. Once a month, they took a big empty hamper with them to give to Cross's, the grocer's, with their order. At the end of the day, the grocer sent us back the hamper, full of food, by train.

While father went to the York cattle market, mother went shopping. I loved going with her. My favourite shop was the Penny Bazaar. Everything was laid out in rows on big counters. There were thimbles and cotton reels, little dolls with china heads and stuffed bodies, tin whistles and tiny tin toys, and sweets such as toffees and humbugs.

Advertisement hoardings in York in 1913.

On special occasions we went to Terry's restaurant. Downstairs they served lunches and dinners. Upstairs were the tea-rooms.

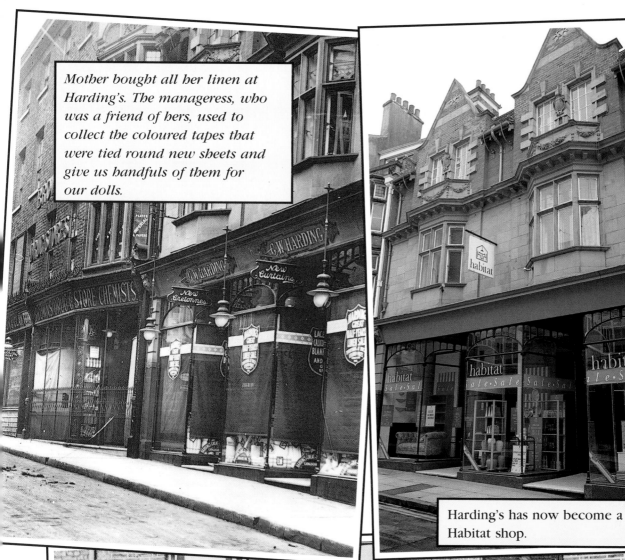

Mother bought all her linen at Harding's. The manageress, who was a friend of hers, used to collect the coloured tapes that were tied round new sheets and give us handfuls of them for our dolls.

Harding's has now become a Habitat shop.

This was my favourite shop.

Sundays

"He would fetch out his watch"

On Sundays, we went to church both morning and evening. Father was one of the church wardens. We sat with our grandfather in the front pew directly below the pulpit.

Grandfather was a rich farmer, who rather thought of himself as the local squire. When he went out, he always dressed very smartly in a frock coat and a silk hat and had a big pocket-watch. If he felt the sermon was going on too long, he would fetch out his watch as a signal to the vicar to stop.

'Dadda', my grandfather, Henry Quarton Gillah.

The church at Wilberfoss.

After father's death, we girls paid for a new pair of church gates in his memory.

TO THE GLORY OF GOD AND IN LOVING MEMORY OF ARTHUR GEORGE GILLAH FOR MANY YEARS CHURCHWARDEN OF THIS PARISH THESE GATES ARE GIVEN BY HIS DAUGHTERS A.D. 1936

My grandmother, Ann Sherbourne, and her grandchildren at Newton Lodge.

The Methodist Chapel has now been converted into a private house.

Emma and Rachel Sherbourne, Mrs Sherbourne's great-great-grandchildren, now live at Newton Lodge. They are the fifth generation of Sherbournes to live there.

On Sunday afternoons, we went to Sunday School. There was no Sunday School for our church so we went to the Methodist Sunday School instead. Every week, I learned a poem off by heart.

Afterwards, I went to visit my grandmother who lived at Newton Lodge, about a mile-and-a-half from Wilberfoss. I walked there on my own. Usually, I took her a piece of cake for her tea and some pale pink wool for her knitting. She used to knit all our vests.

She always wore a black velvet dress and a little white lace hat. She suffered very badly from arthritis, so she lived in one room on the ground floor and had a housekeeper to look after her and the house.

Visitors

"The butcher's boy came every Thursday"

There were always people coming and going to and from our house. Grandfather came to visit regularly. He was very much in charge of the family business. He saw to the family accounts and paid all the bills. When he arrived, we had to wait at the front door and shake hands with him. There was never any kissing. He was a very stern man. I don't remember ever seeing him smile.

Once a week, a fisherman came from Hull with a barrel of herring on his cart. The butcher's boy came every Thursday to take our weekly order. My father always ordered a 10lb piece of beef for Sunday dinner, which we had cold on Mondays.

A chimney-sweep with his brushes.

My grandfather and aunt Lillie outside our house in their gig. My aunt looked after grandfather when my grandmother died, and never married. I didn't know my grandmother. She died before I was born.

Mr Woods delivered groceries from his village shop when we needed them. He brought sugar, tea, biscuits, cocoa, salt and enormous bags of flour. At Christmas, he gave the family a big box of biscuits for being good customers.

Every now and then, a knife-sharpener came with his grinder, to sharpen all our knives and scissors. The coalman came regularly with bags of coal. Once a year, a chimney-sweep came to clean the chimneys. We used to wait outside to watch the brush come out of the top of the chimney.

Who says BOVRIL?

We bought only foods that we could not grow or make ourselves.

A travelling knife-sharpener.

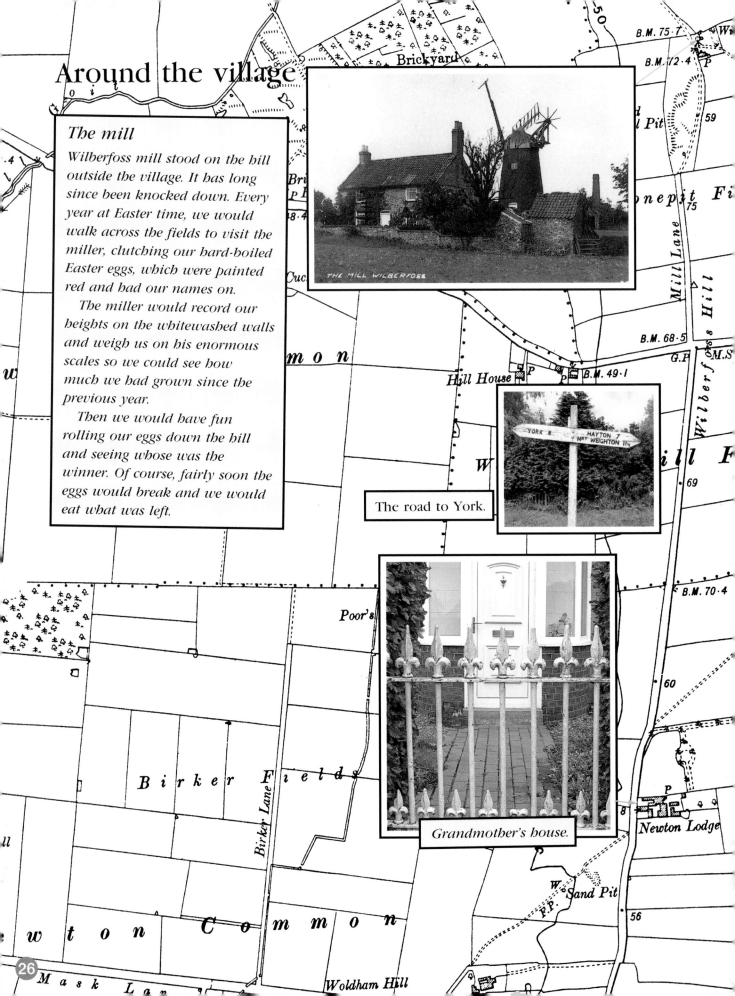

The mill

Wilberfoss mill stood on the hill outside the village. It has long since been knocked down. Every year at Easter time, we would walk across the fields to visit the miller, clutching our hard-boiled Easter eggs, which were painted red and had our names on.

The miller would record our heights on the whitewashed walls and weigh us on his enormous scales so we could see how much we had grown since the previous year.

Then we would have fun rolling our eggs down the hill and seeing whose was the winner. Of course, fairly soon the eggs would break and we would eat what was left.

THE MILL WILBERFOSS

The road to York.

Grandmother's house.

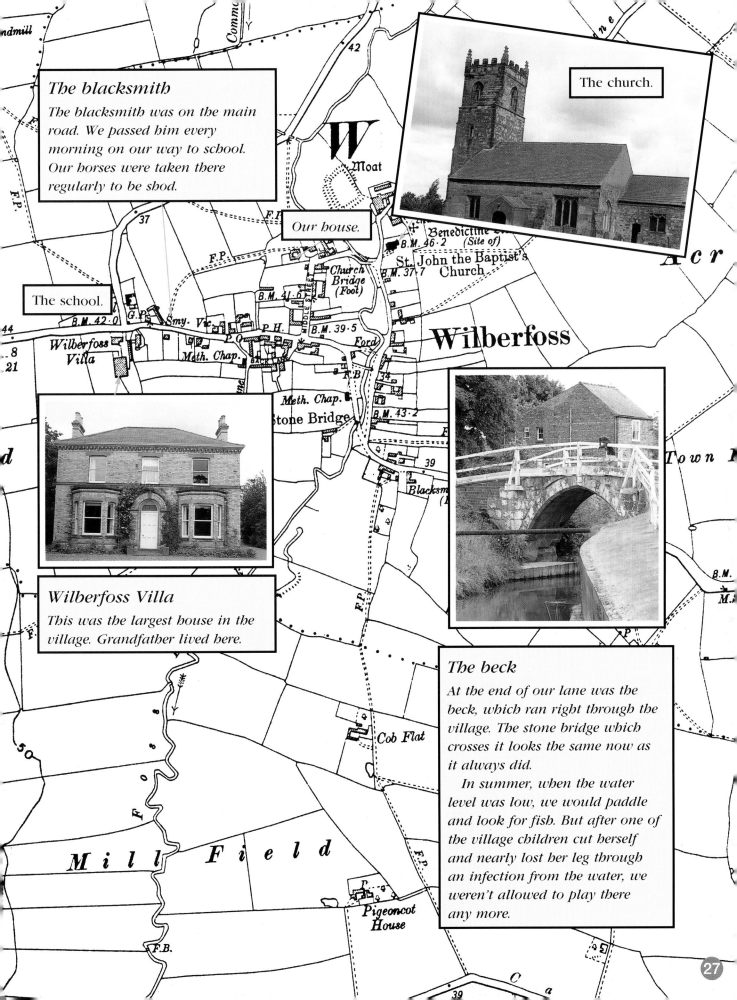

The blacksmith

The blacksmith was on the main road. We passed him every morning on our way to school. Our horses were taken there regularly to be shod.

The church.

Our house.

The school.

Wilberfoss Villa

This was the largest house in the village. Grandfather lived here.

The beck

At the end of our lane was the beck, which ran right through the village. The stone bridge which crosses it looks the same now as it always did.

In summer, when the water level was low, we would paddle and look for fish. But after one of the village children cut herself and nearly lost her leg through an infection from the water, we weren't allowed to play there any more.

School

"No talking was allowed"

As soon as we were old enough to go to school, we walked there by ourselves. We were lucky, the school wasn't far from our house. Some children had to walk a mile or more to get there.

There were three classrooms — one for infants, one for the middle class and a big room for the oldest children. The headmaster, Mr Andrews, taught the oldest children. He was very strict. No talking was allowed. If you were bad, you had to come out and stand in front of the whole class. If it was really serious, you had to hold out your hand for the cane. It didn't hurt too much.

The schoolyard was divided by a wall. The girls came into school by the garden gate and the boys by the main gate. It was funny really. Although boys and girls were taught in the same class, we played in separate playgrounds with that wall between us.

Me and my younger sisters dressed for school. Our sailor suits were navy blue and we wore ankle boots which buttoned all the way up the side.

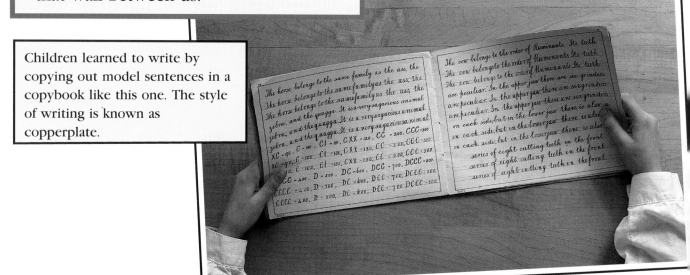

Children learned to write by copying out model sentences in a copybook like this one. The style of writing is known as copperplate.

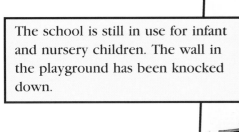

The school is still in use for infant and nursery children. The wall in the playground has been knocked down.

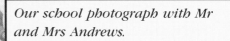

Our school photograph with Mr and Mrs Andrews.

Children sat at desks arranged in rows. The desks each had an inkwell and a groove for keeping a pen.

We started the day in the big room. We sang a hymn and said a prayer. The little children learned to write by drawing their letters in a sand tray. When you were older, you used dip pens with ink. I remember we had to learn our tables off by heart and recite poetry. We did modelling with dark-green Plasticine, and the older girls learned to sew and knit.

There were no school dinners. We went home for ours, but children who lived too far away brought theirs. In winter, Mrs Andrews made a hot drink and the children sat round the coal fire in the schoolroom to eat.

"Sure I was meant to be a teacher"

When I was eleven, I went to school in York. My eldest sister was a teacher and she was sure I was meant to be a teacher too, so she persuaded my parents to send me to the Queen Anne's School for girls. We had to work hard there, but I enjoyed it.

Our class moved to Mill Mount School when Queen Anne's became overcrowded and I stayed there until I was 17 and took my school certificate.

The Mill Mount School buildings still stand, but they have been taken over by All Saints' Comprehensive School.

At Queen Anne's, pupils wore a navy blue tunic, a school blouse, a tie, black stockings and gym shoes. This is the hockey team in 1917.

My youngest sisters went to a different school, but it was also in York, so we travelled together. We had to cycle two miles to Fangfoss and then take a train to York. Father had a little shed built at the station where we could leave our bikes.

The railway at Fangfoss was closed in 1965 and the rails were removed. The station is now a private home and the land around it is used as a caravan park.

The train from Fangfoss to York.

The railway station at York.

High days and holidays

"Our own amusements"

After school and during the holidays, we made our own amusements. We didn't have many toys, although we younger ones each had a doll. We had a doll's pram that was handed down to each of us in turn. By the time it reached Mary, the youngest, it had lost its hood.

Sometimes we played with marbles — coloured clay ones or glass ones — which were great treasures. We also skipped to nursery rhymes, played hopscotch and rolled hoops. I had a metal hoop, but Joyce and Mary had only wooden ones.

Every week, when mother came back from York, she would bring us comics to read — *Comic Cuts, Rainbow,* the *Children's Newspaper* and *Puck,* my favourite. At Christmas, I usually got a *Blackie's Children's Annual,* as a present, which was a big treat.

Doll's prams were small replicas of prams of the time.

1D PUCK

TRESPASSERS ARE REQUESTED NOT TO

No. 49. Vol. II.

EVERY FR

JOHNNY JONES HAS SOME SPORT, AND THE

In springtime, we used to go to the pond and look for tadpoles. We used to say that Ginny Greenteeth would pull you in if you went too near.

Once a year, there was a village social. We dressed in our best clothes and there was a fancy-dress parade. In July, there was a Sunday School treat. The children had a huge tea and some of us were given books as prizes for our work.

Christmas was a family affair. Mother made the Christmas pudding and cake and hung up our stockings. She always cooked a Christmas dinner for Mrs Blackburn and her four children as well as one for us.

Everybody dressed up for the fancy-dress parade.

"We never went swimming in the sea"

We always went to Scarborough for two weeks' summer holiday. Mother, father and we four youngest girls, plus Edith, one of the maids, travelled there by train. My father, for some reason, stayed on his own in an hotel, while the rest of us stayed in a rented house. Packing was an enormous task. We took a great hamper of food with us, which included a whole home-cooked ham.

There were two big beaches to play on. We wore cotton gingham dresses which we tucked into matching knickers when we went paddling. We never went swimming in the sea. There was a small open-air swimming pool, but the water was always freezing, so we didn't enjoy that very much.

For special treats, we were bought rock and humbugs, which we tried to make last as long as we could.

Our favourite beach was Children's Corner. It was flat and sandy — perfect for making sandcastles.

There were entertainments on the beach. Pierrots sang funny songs and told jokes. There were also Punch and Judy shows and donkey rides.

PIERROTS, SCARBOROUGH

When the First World War broke out, Scarborough was bombarded by a German ship and there was a lot of damage.

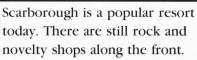

Scarborough is a popular resort today. There are still rock and novelty shops along the front.

Railways offered cheap bargain tickets to the seaside in advertisements like this.

Growing up

"Never the same at home again"

When I was 16, my mother died. I thought it was the end of the world. Things were never the same again at home. At first, my sister, Kathleen, took over the running of the house, but father didn't expect any of us to give up our life to look after him. He remarried a woman with two grown-up daughters and a young son. They bought a car, a Buick, and had a bathroom put in the house, but it was not a happy marriage.

The same year, my sister, Marjorie, got married and Sylvia and I were her bridesmaids.

Mother and father were buried together in Wilberfoss churchyard.

Our 1926 Buick.

Marjorie's wedding. Our bridesmaids' dresses were a soft shade of purple taffeta.

COPY.

South Dalton.

October 10th 1927.

Miss N.E.Gillah taught in this school from December 1925 to August 1927 in the Infants' Department.

She proved herself capable and efficient and took a keen interest in her work. She was a good disciplinarian and won the confidence and affection of the children.

She took charge of the needlework for all classes with very successful results.

She was punctual and always ready to further the interests and maintain the high moral tone of the school.

(sgd) B.F.Atkinson.

(Headmistress).

The reference from one of the schools where I taught.

I was married in 1931, in Bombay Cathedral.

Me aboard s.s. Rampura, *bound for Bombay, India.*

I left school the following year and became a pupil infant teacher, so I could save enough money to pay for a college training. In those days, there were no grants or loans. I taught in two local schools for two years and then went to college in London.

In the summer I finished my training, I met my husband-to-be. He was just about to sail to India to a new job. Two years later, I sailed out to India to marry him.

In the news

These are some of the important events that made news during Nancy's childhood.

1908 Henry Ford, an American, produced the first cheap, mass-produced car, known as the Model T.

1908 onwards. Suffragettes in Britain held rallies and demonstrations, demanding the vote for women. Many women went to prison.

1909 Robert Peary, an American explorer, was the first to reach the North Pole.

1909 Bleriot, a Frenchman, made the first Channel crossing in an aeroplane.

1841   1910

IN MEMORIAM

1910 The British king, Edward VII, died and was succeeded by George V.

1911 Roald Amundsen, a Norwegian, was the first person to reach the South Pole. He beat a British expedition, led by Captain Scott, by five weeks. Scott and his party all died on their return journey.

1912 The *Titanic* liner sank on her maiden voyage across the Atlantic with the loss of 1,513 lives.

1914 The Panama Canal opened. This 50-mile waterway linked the Atlantic and Pacific Oceans and saved ships the long, dangerous journey of 6,000 miles around the tip of South America.

1914 Outbreak of World War I. The Allies (Britain and its Empire, France, Italy, Russia and the United States) fought the Central Powers (which included Germany, Austria-Hungary and Turkey). After four years, the Allies won.

1917 The Tsar of Russia was overthrown. The Bolshevik Revolution, led by Lenin, began the process of turning Russia into a Communist state.

1919 The first non-stop trans-Atlantic flight was made by Alcock and Brown.

1918 Women in Britain over the age of thirty got the vote.

Things to do

Make your own family tree

See if you can trace your own family back to the turn of the century. The easiest way to do this is to make an outline like this and fill in the details as you discover them.

GREAT-GRANDPARENTS

name ....
b. ....
birthplace ....
job ....
m. ....
d. ....
d. where ....

name ....
b. ....
birthplace ....
job ....
d. ....
d. where ....

GRANDPARENTS

name ....
b. ....
birthplace ....
job ....
m. ....
d. ....
d. where ....

name ....
b. ....
birthplace ....
job ....
m. ....
d. ....
d. where ....

name ....
b. ....
birthplace ....
job ....
d. ....
d. where ....

PARENTS

name ....
b. ....
birthplace ....
job ....
m. ....

name ....
b. ....
m. ....
birthplace ....
job ....
d. ....
d. where ....

name ....
b. ....
birthplace ....
job ....
m. ....
d. ....
d. where ....

name ....
b. ....
birthplace ....
job ....
d. ....
d. where ....

MYSELF
b. ....
birthplace ....

name ....
b. ....
birthplace ....
job ....
m. ....
d. ....
d. where ....

name ....
b. ....
birthplace ....
job ....
d. ....
d. where ....

name ....
b. ....
birthplace ....
job ....

name ....
b. ....
birthplace ....
job ....
d. ....
d. where ....

name ....
b. ....
birthplace ....
job ....
m. ....
d. ....
d. where ....

name ....
b. ....
birthplace ....
job ....
d. ....
d. where ....

name ....
b. ....
birthplace ....
job ....
d. ....
d. where ....

Use the following abbreviations to save space:

b.	born
d.	died
=	married
d. unm.	died unmarried
dau.	daughter
s.	son
m.	date of marriage

Maps

You can see how a village or town has changed over time by looking at old maps. Most reference libraries or local archives have old maps, copies of which can usually be supplied.

Compare the roads and the number of buildings. See if you can find schools, Post Offices, pubs, churches and chapels and other landmarks on an old map and notice whether they are still in the same places on a modern map.

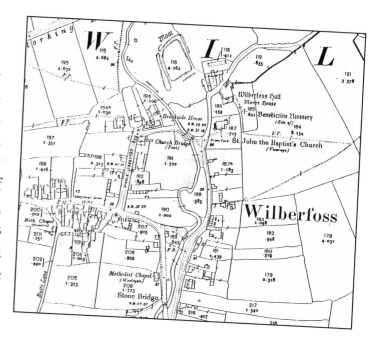

Pictures

Ask your relatives if they have any old family photographs, magazines or post-cards you could look at. Ask them to tell you what they remember about them. If you are allowed to borrow any, look after them carefully and keep them in a safe place, because they are irreplaceable.

Family photographs were not as common in Nancy's childhood as they are now. Very few people had cameras of their own. Some families went to a studio to be photographed. Notice how stiff and formal people look in most of these pictures.

In Nancy's childhood, postcards were extremely popular. They showed famous people of the time, special events, topical cartoons and typical transport, as well as street scenes and views. You can find out a great deal about the fashions, interests and events of the time by studying postcards. Look in junk shops for original old cards and in museum shops and stationers for reproductions.

On the Spa, Scarborough

Glossary

Beck
A small stream.

Chamber pot
A large china pot, kept in a bedroom for use as a toilet, particularly at night. Very common at a time when most toilets were outside.

Churn
A wooden barrel or tub used for butter-making.

Copper
A large, cylindrical tub made of copper or iron, set in brickwork with a fire underneath, used for heating water.

Copybook
A writing book showing how each letter of the alphabet is shaped. Children used to learn to write by copying letters and sentences in such books.

Dairy
A place where milk is kept and butter and cheese are made. Usually a cool, north-facing room with a stone floor.

Drover
A person employed to walk cattle from one place to another.

Eiderdown
A quilt for a bed, stuffed with feathers.

Frock-coat
A double-breasted, full-skirted coat worn by men.

Gig
A light, horse-drawn, four-wheeled carriage, with a big hood, which holds two people.

Gingham
A kind of cotton cloth, woven in coloured stripes or checks.

Gleaning
Gathering handfuls of corn left behind after reaping.

Hamper
A large basket, often made of wicker.

Hoarding
A large board used for displaying advertisements.

Maiden voyage
The first journey made by a ship.

Mangle
A large metal upright frame with two or three wooden rollers set in it. Used for squeezing water out of wet washing and smoothing it.

Mass-produced
Made in great quantity.

Pew
A fixed wooden bench in a church.

Pocket-watch
A small, strapless watch, often carried in a waistcoat pocket, and attached to the waistcoat by a chain.

Poss-tub
A steel or zinc tub used for clothes washing. Also known as a dolly-tub in some parts of Britain. Many had a reinforced rim to catch any water spilt when the clothes were being thumped up and down with a poss-stick.

Pulpit
A raised platform with a bookrest found near the front of a church, used for preaching from.

Range
A coal-fired stove made of iron, with ovens built into the sides and a hot surface on top for saucepans and kettles.

School Certificate
An examination taken by children in their last year of schooling.

Squire
An English or Irish gentleman who owns a great deal of land. The land has often been inherited from titled or wealthy ancestors.

Stackyard
A yard in which large built-up piles of hay, corn and wood are stored.

Suffragettes
Women who campaigned for the right of all women to vote in general elections.

Thatch
A roof made of straw, heather, reeds or similar natural materials.

Trap
A four-wheeled horse-drawn carriage, which holds four people.

Wash-house
An outbuilding which housed a copper and in which washing equipment was kept.

Index

Advertising 14, 20, 25, 35
Alcock 41
allies 40
Amundsen, Roald 39

Bathing 14
beck 27
blacksmith 27
Bleriot 39
Bolshevik Revolution 41
Brown 41
butcher 16, 24
butter-making 10, 13

Cattle dealers 16
chamber pot 11
Channel crossing (first) 39
chimney-sweeping 24, 25
church 22, 27
clothes-horse 12
coach-house 11
coal fire 11
coalman 25
coal-store 11
comics 32, 33
cooking 11, 13, 14
copper, the 11, 12, 14
copperplate 28
copybooks 28
cowshed 10, 11
cutters 16

Dairy 10
Driffield 16
drinkings 18
drovers 16

Edward VII 8, 39
eiderdowns 15, 18
electricity 10, 11

Family tree 9
Fangfoss 31
farming 18, 19, 22
fisherman 24
food 10, 15, 18, 20, 24, 25, 33, 35
Ford, Henry 38

Gardens and gardening 10, 12, 15, 18
gas lighting 11
George V 39

gig 11, 24
gleaning 19
grocer 20, 25

Habitat 21
Hardings 21
holidays 32, 33, 34
housekeeper 23
housework 14
Hull 24

Ironing 13

Kitchen 10, 13, 14
knife-grinder 25

Lavatory 11
Lenin 41

Maids 10, 14, 15, 34
Malton 16
mangle 12, 13
maps 26, 27, 43
market fairs 16, 17, 20
Marks and Spencer 21
Model-T 38
miller 26

Newton Lodge 23
nits 14
North Pole 38

Oil-lamps 11
outbuildings 11, 12

Panama Canal 40
Peary, Robert 38
Penny Bazaars 20, 21
pickers 18
pigsty 11, 18
plucking (geese) 15
pocket-watch 22
possers 12
poss-tub 12
pump 11, 12

Railway 31
range 10, 13

Sacking 11
Scarborough 34, 35
school 15, 27, 28, 29, 30, 31, 37

Scott, Captain 39
shopping 20, 21
squire 22
South Pole 39
stables 10, 11
stacks 19
suffragettes 38
Sunday school 23, 33

Terry's Restaurant 20
tie-pin 16
Titanic, the 40
toothcomb 14
toys 20
trap 11, 20
trans-atlantic flight (first) 41
Tsar of Russia 41

Uniforms (maids) 14

Wash-house 10, 11, 12, 14, 15,
washing 11, 12, 13
wash-stands 11
watch-chain 16
water tanks 11
Wilberfoss 8, 16, 23, 26, 27, 36
women's vote 41
World War I 17, 18, 35, 40

York 8, 16, 20, 26, 30, 31, 32
Yorkshire 16
Yorkshire Post, The 16

A. W. G.'s Celebrated Mangling and Wringing Machines.

The "Gamage."
No. 18.

Rollers, 20 in. by 6 in., Brass Caps	£2 2 6
,, 21 in. by 6 in. ,,	2 3 9
,, 22 in. by 6 in. ,,	2 4 9
,, 24 in. by 6 in. ,,	2 6 9
,, 27 in. by 6 in. ,,	2 13 6

Superior Quality. Fine Polished Rollers.

Extra Powerful Springs.

NO BETTER MANGLE MADE AT ANY PRICE.

Broken in Transit.—Should any Machine be broken by the Railway Company or Carriers, it should be returned to us at once, marked "Carriage Free, Broken in Transit," and an advice forwarded by Post.

The "Holborn."
No.

Best Value ever offered.

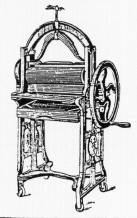

Rollers, 18 in. by 5¼ in.	33/9
,, 20 in. by 5¼ in.	34/6
, 21 in. by 5¼ in.	34/9
,, 22 in. by 5¼ in.	35/-
24 in. by 5¼ in.	35/6

Equal quality. Cannot be bought elsewhere except at 25 per cent. over these prices.

BEST LONDON MAKE.

Selected Maple Rollers.

Every Machine Guaranteed.

OUR SPECIAL LEADING LINE.

The "Beatorl" Mangle.

Remarkable Value. Guaranteed throughout. This Mangle has been placed on the Market to meet the demand for a cheap but serviceable Mangle, and we are confident of its giving every satisfaction.
Made in One Size only, 18 in. by 5 in. Selected Rollers.

Price **27/9**

BEST LONDON MAKE.

With Brass Caps, 1/6 extra.

Absolutely the Cheapest Mangle on the Market.

Free delivery in London District.

Country and Abroad carriage forward.

The "Gamage" Improved Table Mangle.

The "Gamage" is the most cleverly designed Table Mangle in existence. Being small, compact, and light, it can easily be stowed away after use; yet is in every way an absolutely efficient machine, and so strong as to be almost unbreakable. Every part is carefully made and thoroughly tested. The New Lever Handle in place of a balance wheel—saves space, and works with the greatest ease.

When reversed, it is not only out of the way, but also forms a Safety Lock to prevent the cogs and rollers from turning. The "Gamage" is, in fact, the Ideal Machine for every house where space is valuable.

Best Quality Rollers:

16 in. by 3½ in. **18/11**   18 in. by 3½ in. **19/11**   20 in. by 3½ in. **21/-**

Delivered Free within London Radius.

Country and Abroad Carriage Forward.

Every part of this little Machine is strong and durable. The framework is made of wrought iron combined with cast iron. There are four steel spiral springs, and three powerful clamps.

The "New Era" Wringer.

On Ball Bearings.
Standard high grade Rollers.
Steel Springs.
Wheel Pressure Screws.
Extra Large Folding Apron.

Size of Rollers—
10 in.   12 in.   14 in.

	Usual price	Gamage price
10 in.	20/6 ..	**13/11**
12 in.	25/6 ..	**18/9**
14 in.	36/6 ..	**21/-**

All Mangles and Wringers delivered Carriage Free in London.
Outside London carrier radius Carriage forward.

The 'President" Wringer.

This Machine has best tempered steel spring, iron fixing screws, and ACME Rubber Rollers with Cogs on both ends.
Guaranteed for one year—
Fair tear and wear excepted.
To fix on Round or Square Tub or Table.

Order No.			Size of Rollers.			Price
10	..	..	12 in.	..	..	**19/11**
11	..	..	14 in.	..	..	**21/-**
13	..	..	16 in.	..	..	**25/6**

The Gamage Magic Table.

An ingenious but simple combination of Mangle, Wringer, Washing Tank and Table, eminently suitable for flats and small houses, where space is limited. Can be converted into a table, mangle or washing tank in a very few moments. As a **Table**, sides and legs of very strong American maple wood, neatly varnished, whitewood top; really looks like a table. Dimensions 31½ in. height by 34 by 23½ in. As a **Washing Tank**, the tank is constructed of strong galvanised iron, fitted with outlet, plug, &c. As **Mangle** and **Wringer**, entirely new design, compact and practically unbreakable. The tank catches all the drips. Constructed of wrought iron bars embeded in cast iron and fitted with 4 spiral steel springs. Rollers of selected American maple.

Size of rollers, 18 by 3½ in.   Price .. **39/6**

Carriage forward outside London district.

SPECIAL NOTICE.—Price of Rubber Wringers are apt to fluctuate according to the state of the markets.

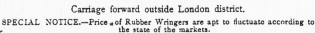

AS A WRINGER & WASHING TANK.   AS A TABLE.

Q 2

The World's Finest Selection and Largest Stock

THE GREAT GROWTH

In the use of Carpet Sweepers during recent years, has caused us to make a distinct feature of the **best brands** on the market. The following is believed to be the best selection of patterns known in the trade.

A Carpet Sweeper has now become a necessity in every household.

THE BENEFIT OF A CARPET SWEEPER

Arises from the ease and speed with which it does the work. It causes neither stooping nor backache, and does not permit any dust to escape into the room. The sweeping is done more thoroughly than that done by a broom under the most favourable conditions; and it is less troublesome, inasmuch as the sweepings are taken right out of the carpet into the machine, and so carried completely away.

Bissell's Ball Bearing 'Parlour Queen.'

Bissell's "Parlour Queen" Carpet Sweeper is all its name implies, and is one of our most highly finished carpet Sweepers. The case of the "Parlour Queen" is made of Rosewood, beautifully figured, and given the highest quality piano polish. All the metal parts are of original design, and well finished in nickel plate.

Our price **20/-** List price 21/-

Bissell's Ball Bearing "Elite."

The "Elite" is a new design in carpet sweepers and combines elegance and richness in style. The case is entirely new in shape, being oval, thus securing artistic effect and at the same time giving the sweeper unusual solidity. The woods used in making the case of the "Elite" are of the choicest, being made in Hungarian Ash, Curly Birch Mahoganized, Brazilian Rosewood and Curly Maple in Seal Brown. The bail and metal ends are also specially designed to harmonize with the artistic lines of the case, all the trimmings being nickelled.

Our price **19/-** List price 20/-

TOY SIZES.

These are delightfully instructive Toys, which sweep in a miniature way, and retain the sweepings like the real machine.

Practically a bye-product of the Bissell factory, and on that account offered at very low prices.

Baby ... 11½d.
The Child's, 1/5½
The Little Queen, 1/11½
The Little Jewel 2/11½

Carpet Sweepers of any make are promptly **repaired** by experts at very moderate charges.

New Brushes, 3/- **New Tyres, 6**d. each
New Tyre-wheel complete ... ... **1**'- ,,

Carpet -- Sweepers

OF

No Home Complete Without One

The Famous **"National"** Roller Bearing Carpet Sweepers at Sweeping Reductions. We WILL Sell Cheaply. Prices again cut for these Great Bargains. Offered at Less than Wholesale Prices.

Absolutely the World's Greatest Value in Carpet Sweepers.

	Our Price.	Elsewhere.
Perpetual, nickeled plated	7/10½	12/0
Perpetual, japanned	6/11½	10/6
Royal Emblem, nickel plated	7/4½	10/6
,, ,, japanned	6/11½	9/9

N.B.—In consequence of the extremely low price, we cannot pay Carriage on these Sweepers. Carriage can be paid by purchaser on delivery.

SPECIAL NOTICE.—The above prices only hold good while the stock last. We hold a good stock, but these are listed on the distinct understanding that when sold they cannot be repeated.

HOTEL SIZES.

These sweepers are especially designed for sweeping large surfaces in Hotels, Halls, Corridors, etc. Being wider than the ordinary sweepers they do the work in much less time. The cases are made of oak.

Bissell's Ball Bearing "Grand."

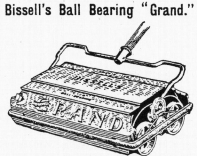

Width over all, 17 inches. Width of Brush, 13½ inches.
Our price ... **23/9** List price **25/-**

Bissell's "Cyco" Bearing 'Club.'

Width over all, 25 inches. Width of Brush, 21 inches.
Our price ... **33/3** List price ... **35/-**

Bissell's "Cyco" Bearing "Hall."

Width over all, 28 inches. Width of Brush, 24½ inches.
Our price ... **40/-** List price ... **42/-**

Bissell's Ball Bearing "Grand Rapids"

The most Popular Sweeper in the World

The "Grand Rapids" Sweeper is now fitted with ball bearings. It runs so easily, a mere touch propels it, and its efficiency as a dust extractor is greatly increased. This sweeper is fitted with our new pressed steel wheels and improved dust-proof axle tube, which ensure free and easy working. The case is made in six assorted choice cabinet woods.

No. 1. With ball bearings and japanned fittings—
Our price **14/3** List price 14/-
No. 2. With ball bearings and nickel fittings—
Our price **15/8** List price 15/6

Bissell's "Cyco" Bearing "Universal."

An old Sweeper under a new name.

Formerly known as our regular "Grand Rapids." Supplied only with "Cyco" Bearings and Japanned Fittings in eight varieties of handsome hardwood. This sweeper combines the best mechanical equipment with the least expensive quality of finish.

Our price ... **13/3** List price ... **14/-**

Bissell's "Cyco" Bearing "Superior."

Nickelled Fittings.

The "Superior" has a single automatic dump for each pan, and contains all improvements such as "Cyco" bearings, dust-proof axle tubes, anti-raveler, reversible bail spring, etc.

Our price ... **14/9** List price ... 15/6

The "Standard." Popular Model

A Strong and Durable Sweeper

The patterns shown on this page have ample power for medium carpets, but like all non-cyco sweepers they cannot tackle the heavy piles for which the cyco bearing movement was created. They are well built, with brushes of pure bristle, and are fully guaranteed

Our price ... **10/6** List price 11/6

The "Crown Jewels" Sweeper,

Similar to above, our price **9/9**